# COLOR YOUR OWN
# Matisse Paintings

## Muncie Hendler

## DOVER PUBLICATIONS, INC.
### Mineola, New York

# NOTE

Henri Matisse was born on December 31, 1869, at Le Cateau in Picardy, France. He first began to paint while recovering from appendicitis when he was 20 years old. In 1891, he abandoned his early studies in law and moved to Paris to become an artist. Matisse attended the Académie Julian and the École des Arts Décoratifs, visited museums, and learned from other painters. In 1898 he married Amélie Parayre and traveled to London and to Corsica, where he was influenced by the Mediterranean sunlight and color. The impact of his trip to the Mediterranean can be seen in many of his works including *The Moorish Café* (page 4).

In 1905 Matisse's works were exhibited at the Salon d'Automne, along with the works of other artists such as Derain and Rouault. Paris critic Louis Vauxcelles called the group *les fauves* ("the wild beasts") for their violent use of color to stir emotions. Matisse was the most famous representative of the movement known as Fauvism. During his career, he also produced murals, book illustrations, sculpture, and collages. In 1941, after being bedridden by an operation, Matisse focused on what he called "drawing with scissors." Working with a crayon attached to a bamboo pole, or directing his assistants on the proper placement of a cutout, Matisse created collages with colored paper. These paper cutouts were first painted with opaque watercolor, a technique called gouache. His book, *Jazz* (1947), is a collection of these collages. Matisse died on November 3, 1954, at Nice, France.

Included in this book are 30 Matisse paintings and cutouts, offering a tantalizing look into the career of one of the greatest artists of the twentieth century. Use your own creativity and imagination to color in these masterpieces, or follow the color schemes used by Matisse (shown on the inside front and back covers).

*Bibliographical Note*

*Color Your Own Matisse Paintings* is a new work, first published by Dover Publications, Inc., in 1998.

*International Standard Book Number: 0-486-40030-1*

Manufactured in the United States of America
Dover Publications, Inc., 31 East 2nd Street, Mineola, N.Y. 11501

1.   **Still Life with "La Danse."** 1909. Oil on canvas.

2.   La Danse. 1909–10. Oil on canvas.

3.    **The Conversation.** 1911. Oil on canvas.

4.   The Moorish Café. 1913. Distemper on canvas.

5.    **Odalisque with a Red Coat.** 1937. Oil on canvas.

6.    **The Dream.** 1940. Oil on canvas.

7. **Icarus.** 1943. Stencil.

8.   Pierrot's Funeral. 1943. Stencil.

9.    The Circus. 1943. Stencil.

10.    **The Clown.** 1943. Stencil.

11.    The Codomas. 1943. Stencil.

12.   **The Toboggan.** 1943. Stencil.

13.    The Horse, the Rider and the Clown. 1943–44. Stencil.

14-15.    **The Thousand and One Nights.** 1950. Gouache cutouts.

. ELLE VIT APPA RAI TRE LE MATIN
ELLE SE TUT DISCRE TEMENT

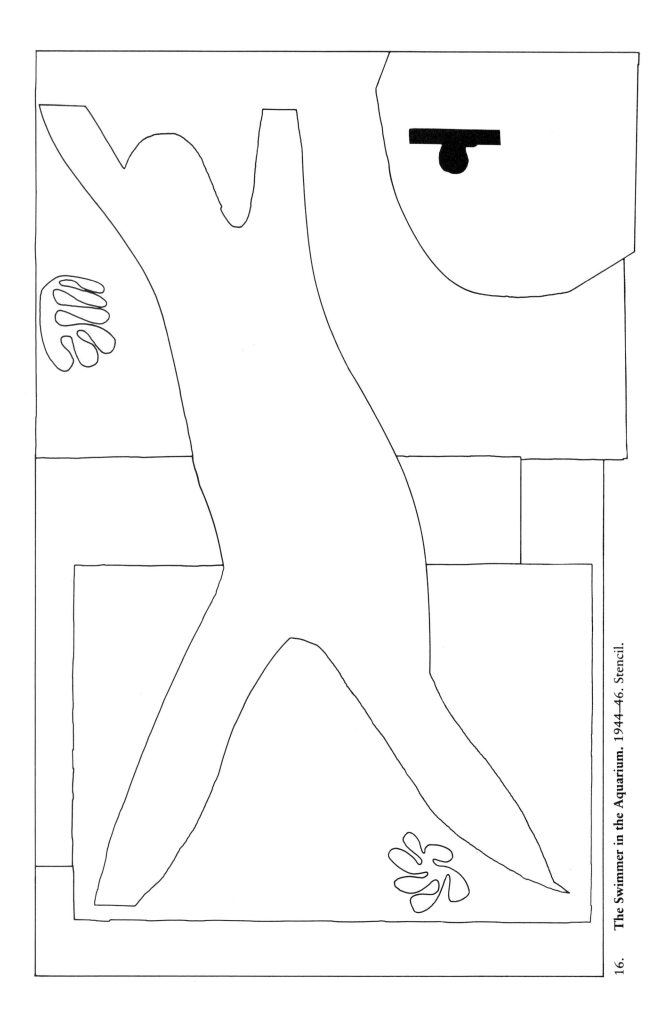

16.    **The Swimmer in the Aquarium.** 1944–46. Stencil.

17. Polynesia, the Sky. 1946. Gouache cutouts.

18.     **Red Interior, Still Life on a Blue Table.** 1947. Oil on canvas.

19.    **Large Red Interior.** 1948. Oil on canvas.

20.    **The Beasts of the Sea.** 1950. Gouache cutouts.

21.  **Creole Dancer.** 1950. Gouache cutouts.

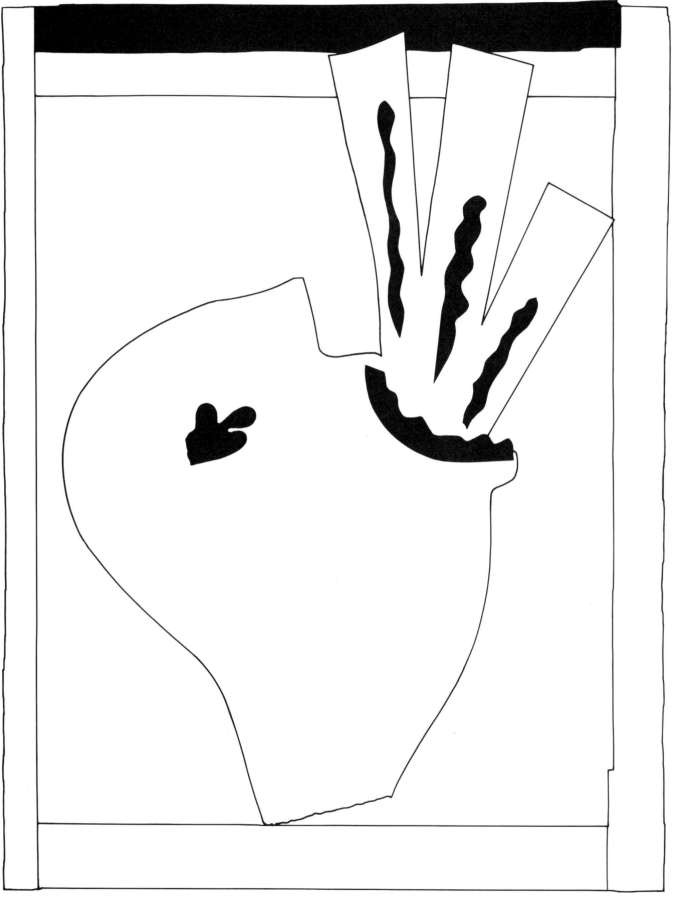

22.    **The Sword Swallower.** 1943–46. Stencil.

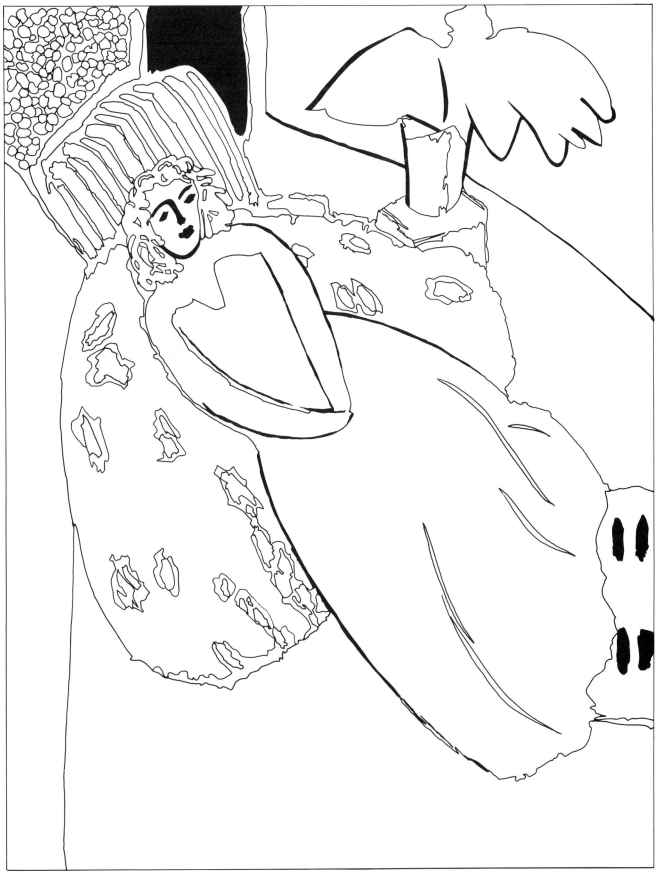

23.    **Young Woman in White, Red Background.** 1944. Oil on canvas.

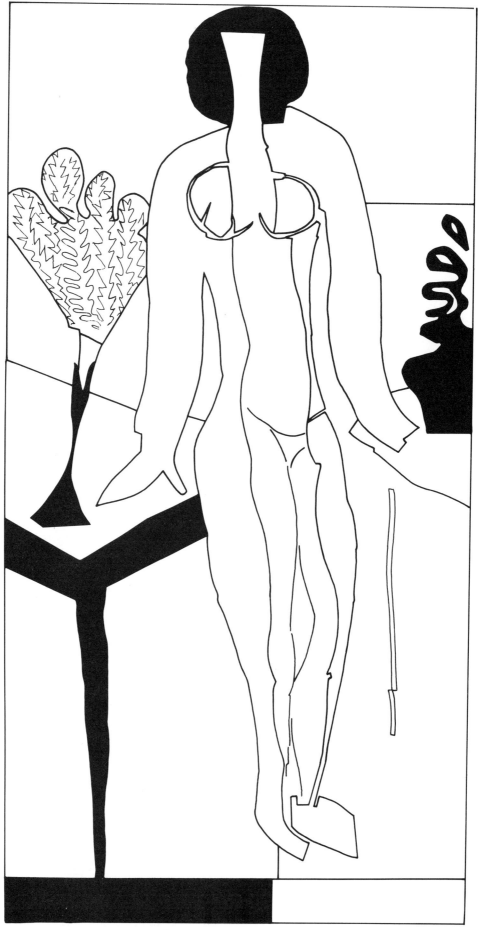

24.    **Zulma.** 1950. Stencil.

25.    **Chinese Fish.** 1951. Gouache cutouts.

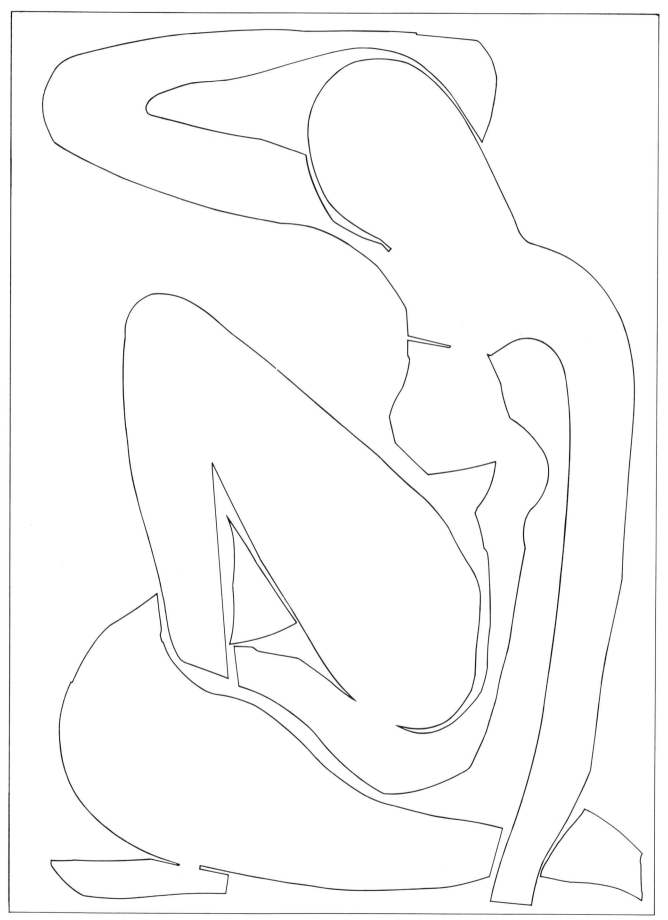

26.    **Blue Nude I.** 1952. Gouache cutouts.

27.    **Nuit de Noël.** 1952. Gouache cutouts.

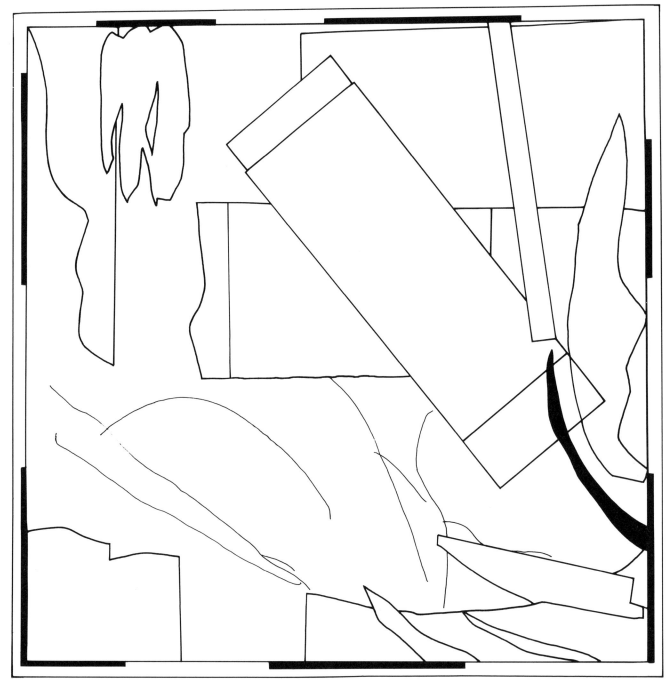

28.    **Memory of Oceania.** 1952–53. Gouache cutouts.

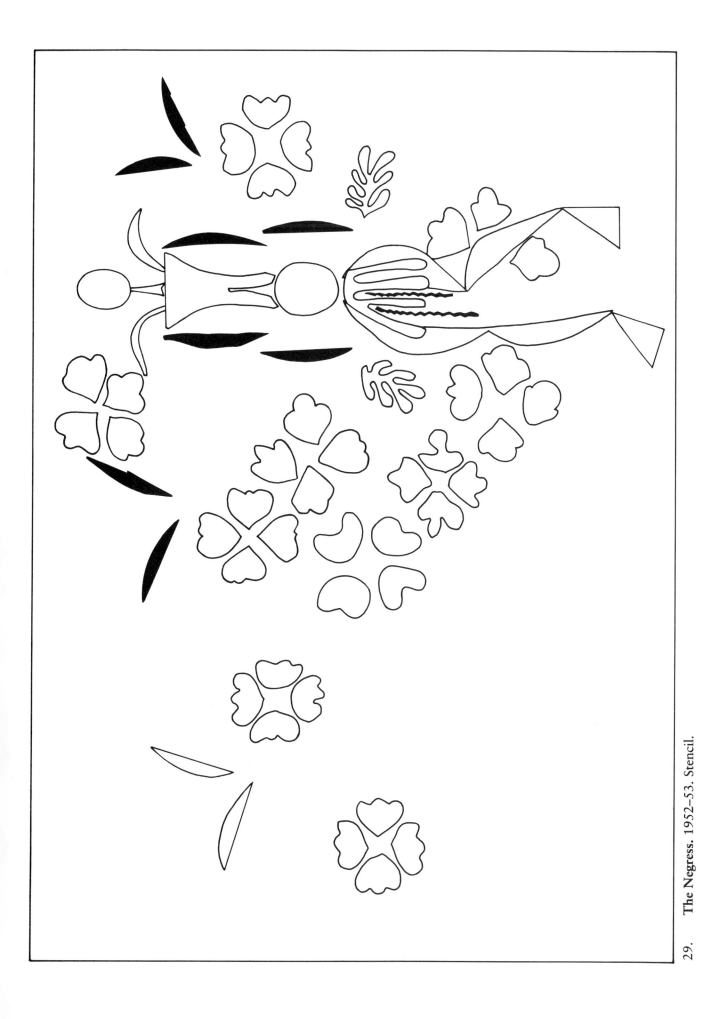

29.   **The Negress.** 1952–53. Stencil.

30.    The Sheaf. 1953. Gouache cutouts.